PORTSMOU

THE OLD TOV. N

Written and Compiled by Peter N. Rogers

HALSGROVE

First published in Great Britain in 2008

British Library Cataloguing-in-Publication Data
A CIP record for this title is available from the British Library

ISBN 978 1 84114 562 4

HALSGROVE
Halsgrove House
Ryelands Industrial Estate, Bagley Road,
Wellington, Somerset TA21 9PZ
Tel: 01823 653777
Fax: 01823 216796
email: sales@halsgrove.com
website: www.halsgrove.com

Printed and bound in Great Britain by
Short Run Press Ltd, Exeter

CONTENTS

A plethora of pages providing a pleasant and profitable pastime for persons peregrinating in pursuit of pleasure, by pointing out each particular prospect and peculiarity of the place.

(Henry Slight – Portsmouth 1837)

To my dear wife to whom I owe all my happiness and any success which I may have achieved in life. I dedicate this book.

PREFACE

A lifelong interest and affection for Old Portsmouth began in those far-off days between the two World Wars when, in the company of my brother and maternal Grandfather, a favourite Sunday walk would take us to the old town where we boys would be regaled with tales pre-dating even the childhood of Grandfather! It was during these occasional excursions that we learned of our ancestors who, at various times had lived in St Mary's, Pembroke and Oyster Streets; a thrill indeed to realise that we were descended from folk who had been citizens of this colourful and ancient town. In our young minds we had considered this proud, though tenuous, connection to be almost a right to citizenship ourselves, such was our desire to be associated with the old town and its history.

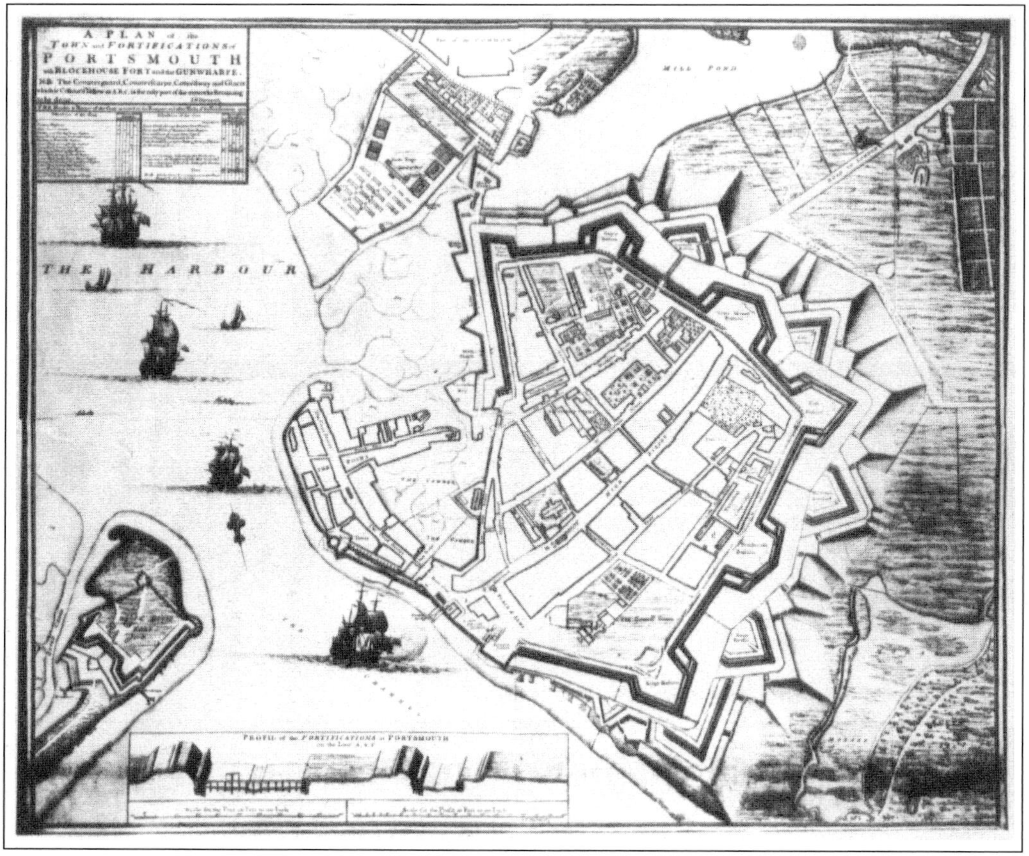

Plan of Portsmouth dated 1745/1750, by Military Engineer, John Peter Desmaretz.

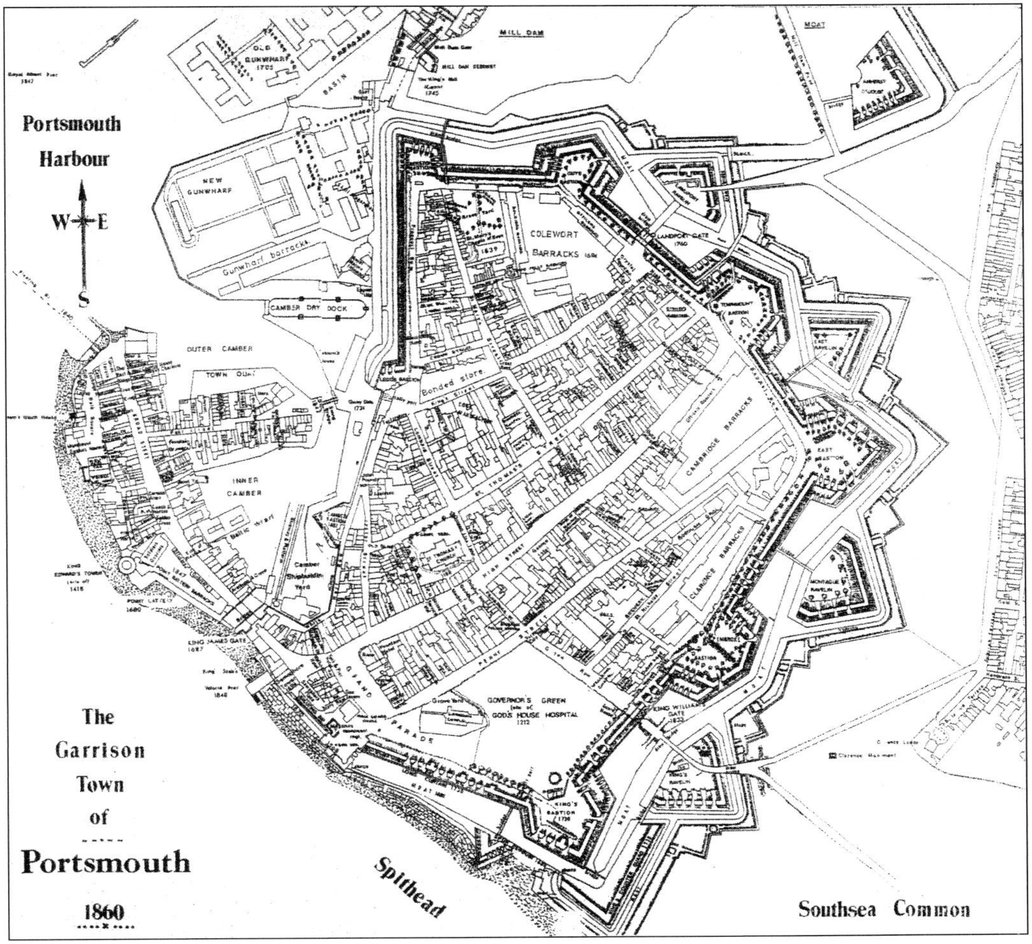

Plan, Garrison Town of Portsmouth, 1860.

ACKNOWLEDGEMENTS

The original sources of the illustrations within these pages are many and the author wishes to express his gratitude to the contributors in general and to friends and colleagues, particularly those in the Portsmouth City Museums and Records Service, Havant Museum and the Hampshire County Museums Service.

My thanks to Brian Patterson for allowing his detailed maps of Old Portsmouth to be reproduced in this volume and to contributions from: David Lewis, Anthony Triggs, Russell Fox, Douglas Sharp, David Francis and the late Mr K.Biles also the late Bill Buckley, Trevor Keys, archivist to the Y.H.A. and David Moss of the *Grimsby Telegraph*.

Grateful thanks also to *The News*, Portsmouth, and to Mr Geoffrey Elliot who, during his time as editor of *The News*, Portsmouth, generously granted permission for illustrations from that publication to be reproduced, and to the Royal Garrison Church and its volunteer guides and researchers, particularly Trevor Gale, Charles Cooper and the late Richard Softley.

Included within these pages are several photographs reproduced from originals, the ownership of which cannot be determined; the author asks forgiveness if he has unwillingly transgressed by using them in this book.

Many of the illustrations are of an age that will exclude them from the copyright act, but, whilst the author has been diligent in his research, there remains the possibility that a particular person or resource has not been acknowledged.

INTRODUCTION

The story of Old Portsmouth as a settled community commences in the last years of the twelfth century, coinciding perhaps with the building of the Church of St Thomas c.1185.

The Domesday Survey of 1086, whilst recording the three manors on Portsea Island, namely Bocheland, Frodintone and Copenor, fails to acknowledge the existence of the town or settlement of Portsmouth. The Great Survey was, of course, introduced as a means of exacting taxes from landowners in general. It could be construed then, that whatever the size of the early settlement which was to become Portsmouth, the population in the year 1086 was possibly too minimal and unimportant for the King's Jurymen to record.

Archaeological evidence however, has revealed the presence of early man along the shores of the sheltered lagoon (today's Camber) from the Neolithic to the early Bronze Age 2500 to 1500 B.C. and beyond. It is probable that seasonal visits were at first made by early nomads where-by they could replenish their stocks of wild fowl, fish and shellfish; plentiful no doubt in the then coastal reed beds and marshlands.

From these small beginnings came the first permanent settlement, later developing into an initial village community whose inhabitants found this small corner of Portsea Island a desirable place to put down roots. A safe, sheltered shoreline, afforded by a natural haven, included numerous freshwater springs that were a further inducement to the establishment of a settlement.

In or about the year 1180, John de Gisors, a wealthy Norman merchant and landowner, is credited with being the founder of the new town of Portsmouth on land previously known as Sude Wede (South Wade or South Water). A merchant with land and properties in both France and England he was quick to recognise the potential offered by a sheltered lagoon and the possibility of future facilities from where he could conduct trade with the continent.

Surrounded by the sea and tidal marshlands. It is unlikely that the early town had definable boundaries and several centuries were to pass before the town limits were officially introduced and recorded. In 1828, local historian and chronicler Dr Henry Slight, published the then route, and routine, to be followed by those whose duty it had been to annually 'beat the bounds'.

'First commence at the low-water mark, one hundred paces to the south-east of the Hot Walls (Kings Ravelin); proceed in a northerly direction into the large moat, cross the little moat to the right hand wall of the large moat, proceed along the outer wall to Landport Bridge; then along the wall to nearly opposite the angle formed from the line from Quay (now King George's) Gate, cross the road (by permission) to the King's Mill; follow that line to the Bastion at Mill Gate, mount the Bastion, descend on the opposite side close to the Portcullis, thence in a direct line (intersecting obliquely the Fort Bridge and water) to the centre of the Gun-Wharf large gates, thence in a direct line to the store-keeper's house, halfway through this house, up three steps to the left, proceed in that line; descend three steps to the right, follow the course of entry to the garden fence, thence to the pear tree in the first clerk's garden, thence to a small chimney in the Superintendent's laundry (Mr Spencers's) thence to the angle of the wall, touching the Common Hard.'

Of the numerous books compiled and written on the subject of Portsmouth's history, only one has been previously devoted entirely to the history of Old Portsmouth: *The Charm Of Old Portsmouth* by the late Richard Esmond, published by Gale and Polden in 1958, is now a rarity greatly valued by those fortunate enough to possess a copy. Pocket sized, it proved to be a useful companion both to the visitor discovering the town for the first time and to the student of history. Written in the years following the Second World War, the author was familiar with and introduced the reader to, the effects of Hitler's bombing. An approximate 50% of the old town was destroyed during the raids and a number of Richard Esmond's pen and ink sketches together with accompanying text, illustrate the devastation caused in this tiny, ancient town of less than one mile square!

For a community as small as Old Portsmouth there could, of course, be a limit to the number and variations of photographs and illustrations that have been recorded. The old town however, has contributed a wealth of illustrative material to the archives of the City of Portsmouth and, while it is inevitable that a number of the pictures contained within these pages will have been seen before, there are, equally, a number of previously unpublished items which will be new and unfamiliar. The author apologises for what sometimes appears to be an apparent, but excusable 'overlap' of such illustrations, and wishes to emphasise that this volume is a pictorial compilation dedicated entirely to the town of Old Portsmouth and is in no way intended to be a written history of the town. Numerous books describing the general history of Portsea Island are to be currently found in local bookshops.

Volumes now out of print may be found in libraries and the Portsmouth City Records Office; together they will offer the interested reader the opportunity to further pursue the history of the old town in greater depth.

THE CAMBER

The present-day City of Portsmouth owes its origins to the Camber, a natural haven, which in pre-history, provided sustenance and shelter to our early ancestors.

The plan of c.1542 shows the Camber protected by a natural sand and shingle bar, the result of perhaps thousands of years of long shore drift added to by deposits swept in, and out, of Portsmouth Harbour and the Solent by countless tidal movements. This sand bar, curving in towards the south-western shoreline of Portsea Island, is unrecognisable now as today's Broad Street and the Town Quay.

Interestingly the plan also shows the original grid pattern of streets upon which the present street plan is faithfully based.

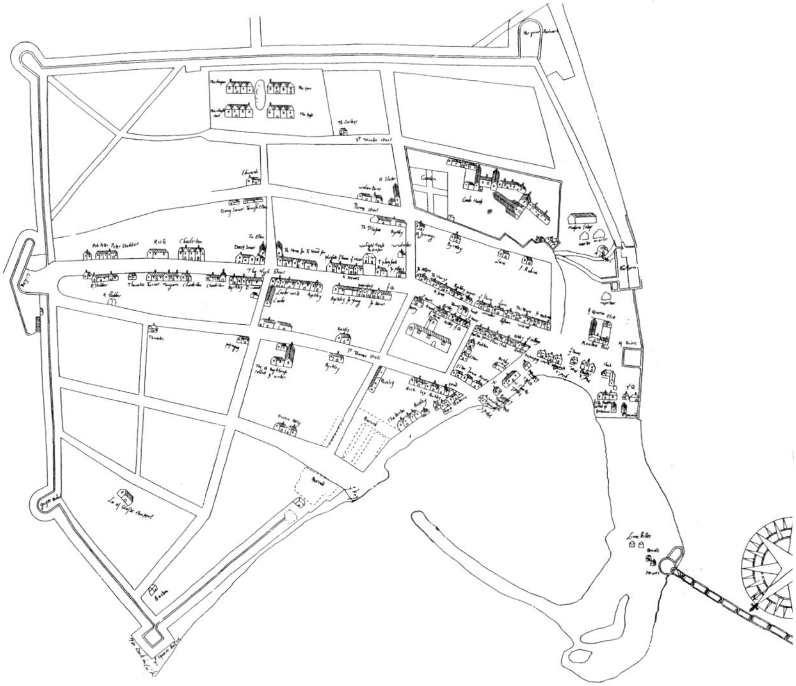

Whilst having no connection with Old Portsmouth, this photograph of the Eastney peninsular at the south-eastern corner of Portsea Island, well illustrates another example of a sand /shingle bar created over many millennia and helping to form Eastney Lake (a perhaps larger version of the Camber). The Eastney shoreline is left to right across the top of the picture whilst Langstone Harbour entrance occupies the lower portion.

Commercial extraction of sand and gravel from the surrounding seaways for the past 200 years has almost put an end to the natural build up of these deposits which have created such phenomena at the entrance to the harbours of the Solent.

An aerial photograph of the Camber dated c.1980 reveals it to be a miniature commercial port. The massive coal storage bunkers of Messrs Fraser and White dominate the dockside together with warehousing, ship's chandlers and Vospers Shipbuilders.

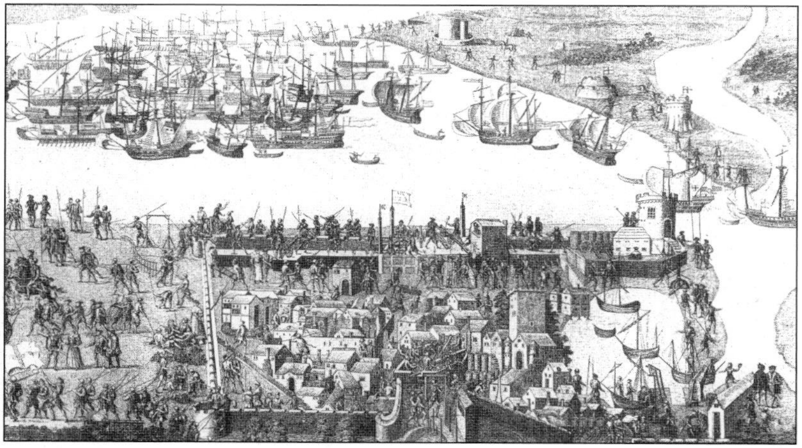

An engraving by James Basire, a small part of which is reproduced here, is from the Cowdray Print, copied from an original painting, which was sadly lost when Cowdray House in Midhurst was destroyed by fire. The painting recorded an attack on Portsmouth by the French on 19 July 1545, the entire work being an important historical source of reference to historians. The western-most section is illustrated to convey to the reader, the shape, size and importance of the Camber Harbour at that time. Shipping is at anchor with additional vessels arriving. Warehousing is built on shore and on piles over the water. The defensive walled town includes both the Round and Square Tower.

In 1915, Messrs Fraser and White installed handling and storage facilities to cater for the huge quantities of seaborne coal now arriving at the Camber. The storage structure of reinforced concrete involving many innovative building methods was 240 feet long by 97 feet wide and could contain 15,000 tons of coal.

Long before Fraser and White began trading, coal was already being brought by sea to be distributed and marketed from the Camber. Here a sailing collier is arriving in Portsmouth Harbour prior to discharging its cargo. Built in Emsworth in 1871 (probably by J.D. Foster), and named *Thorney Island,* the vessel is thought to be a flat-bottomed centre-plate brigantine.

The Camber's Town Quay later became the principal coaling wharf for Portsmouth and the entire local area. In the last years of the nineteenth century, scenes such as this would have been commonplace in Old Portsmouth when small coastal vessels like the *Thorney Island* would ply between ports with cargoes of coal or timber.

Probably recorded from the tower of St Thomas's church c.1870, the photograph reveals how the old town sat at the very edge of Portsmouth Harbour with ships of the Royal Navy providing a backcloth. Surrounded by over-crowded streets, wharfs, warehousing and pubs, the Camber dockside also included the White Hart Barracks (visible bottom left) and an even earlier Camber Bastion.

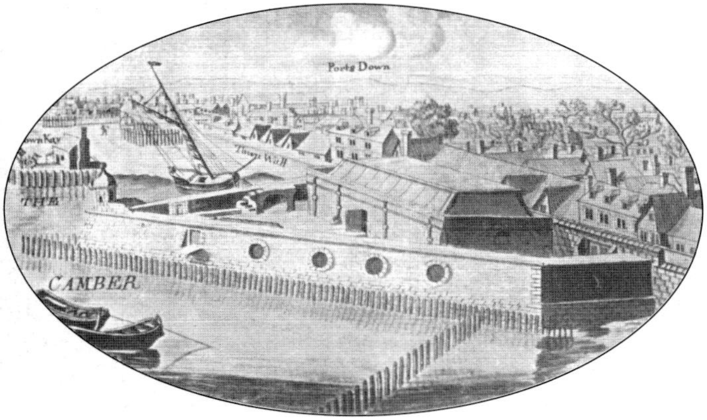

Whilst this engraving is dated 1716, the Camber Bastion had been constructed in the second half of the seventeenth century c.1687. Triangular in shape, it later formed the basis of the White Hart Barracks.

In 1842–43 the inner Camber was deepened and a bascule bridge installed. Additional improvements were made in 1874 and again in 1906 when the bridge was constructed. These two views are of the bridge being raised and in use, followed by its partial demolition in 1923. The Bridge Tavern, seen on the left of Fraser and White's coalbunker, remains today, the only clue as to the one-time location of the bridge and coalbunker.

The severe winter conditions of 1895 were recorded in these views of the Camber on 13 February of that year.

A lone chimney of the recently completed Portsmouth Power Station (1894) contributes to the scene (top left), whilst another view (bottom) features Orange Tree Tavern backing on to East Street; this pub together with its near neighbour, The Ellington, closed for business in 1913.

Above left: With an increasing population and the introduction of street lighting, coupled with the demands of industry and a growing domestic market, the power station constantly needed to increase its output. Pictured in 1927, an additional boiler is being delivered to the site. **Above right:** Following its conversion to a 'wet' dock in 1929, the first collier to arrive with sea-borne coal was the *Earley* carrying a cargo of 1250 tons to be delivered to the generating station by an overhead conveying system of a moving belt.

Below right: On 1 April 1936, the North Sea fishing vessel the *Girl Pat* sailed from Grimsby on a twelve day fishing trip to the North Sea. Captained by skipper 'Dod' Orsborne with a crew of six, the vessel sailed south to Dover! Arriving two days later. She set off two days after that, but then vanished. Nine days later, she was reported as having arrived at the Spanish port of Corcubion. After refuelling and taking on fresh supplies, she set off again heading towards Africa where she was seen in mid-May at Dakar. By now the vessel had been painted white and her name changed to *Kia Ora*. She then set off across the Atlantic. The crew were later arrested at Georgetown British Guiana charged with stealing the vessel.

The story from here on is lengthy; suffice to say that a volunteer crew, making a landfall at Portsmouth's Camber Dock on May 10th 1937, finally brought the *Girl Pat* back to Britain. There had been a nationwide interest in a year-long saga, which had thrilled the world, whilst the excitement generated locally witnessed crowds flocking to the Camber Dock to view the *Girl Pat*.

Courtesy of David Lewis

With the departure of Vospers Shipbuilders in 1985, the Camber no longer caters for ship construction or handling; these rare and unusual c.1860 advertisements however give an insight into the major works, which were once carried out here. In 1861, Thomas White and his family are known to have lived at No.84 St Thomas's Street, sadly one of the many properties destroyed by the bombing of the Second World War.

The eldest son of Thomas White who founded the well-know shipbuilders at Cowes in the Isle of Wight, originated his own company at nearby Gosport before crossing the harbour to establish his business at Portsmouth.

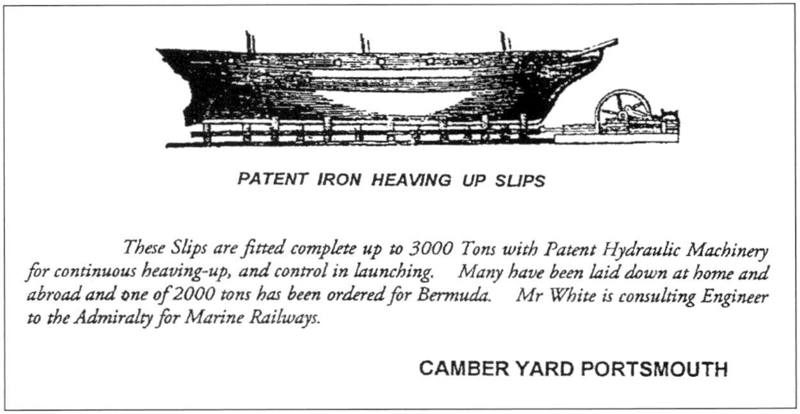

It seems unlikely that the maximum loads advertised could have been handled within the confines of the Camber harbour.

A TOWN DEFENDED

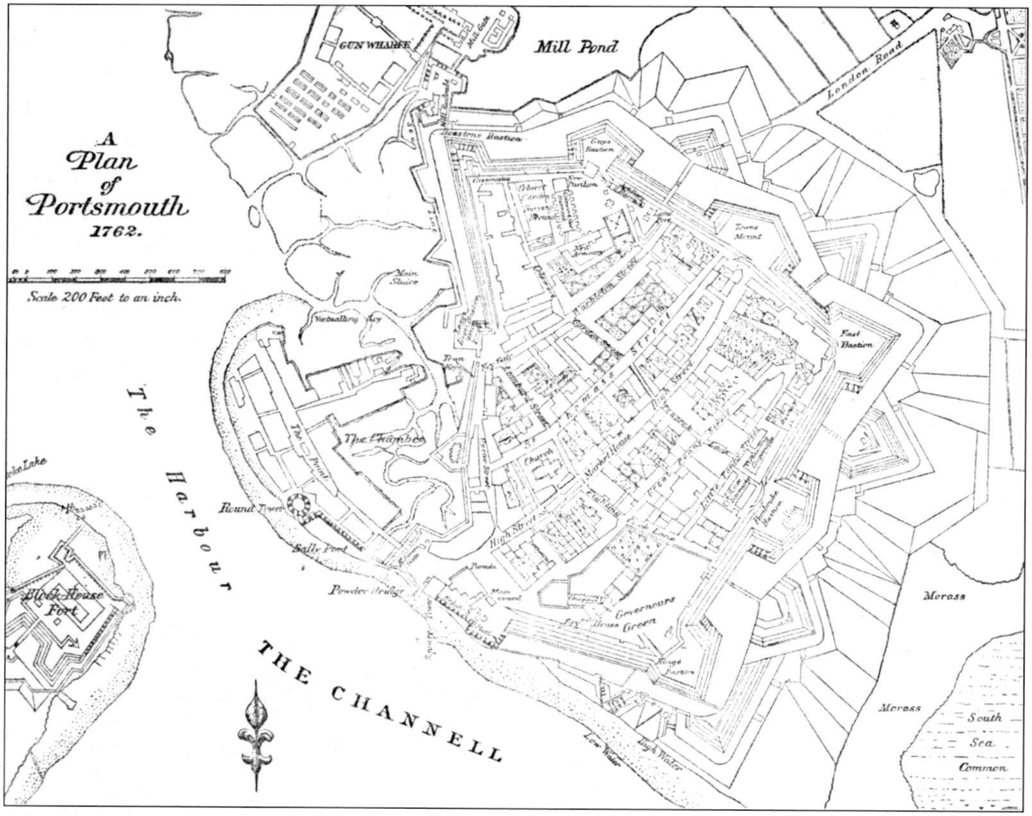

A plan of Portsmouth c.1762, shows the town surrounded by a complex system of strong walls, bastions, ramparts, ravelins, redoubts and water-filled moats; access to the town being afforded by three and later four, gates.

The earliest of the defences, the Round Tower, was commenced c.1417, to defend both the town and entrance to Portsmouth Harbour following at least four raids by the French in the latter half of the fourteenth century; raids in which the town was burned and pillaged. The threat of these incursions and the constant interruption of trade and commerce all but ruined the port. Had it not been for its own agricultural and fishing activities, the little town would have altogether perished.

The building of yet more defensive walls on the seaward shore continued throughout the 15th century, culminating with the construction of the Square Tower c.1494. It will be noticed that Broad Street and Portsmouth Point beyond King James's Gate, were considered to be on 'Spice Island' and as such, isolated from the upper class properties and residents of the town after curfew each evening!

King James's Gate built across Broad Street c.1687, was the most decorative of the gates and supported a heavy drawbridge, which could be lowered across a narrow water inlet feeding the Camber from the sea, thus creating an 'island' community.

The steps giving access to the present pedestrian walkway on top of the old Eighteen Gun Battery defensive wall, are supported by the remains of the structure, to which was attached the King James' Gate; it was at this point that the gate was sited across Broad Street.

Access to the town from Portsea Island could be gained only by passing through one of three original gates. Pictured, is the principal entrance to the town, the Landport or Town, Gate built c.1760 and the only one remaining in situ.

King George's Gate (known also as Quay Gate or Key Gate) was the largest of the town gates. 'A noble structure, rustic in style, adorned with massive pillars and entablature of grand proportions.' Above it, the offices of the Governor and, on the inner side, a large guard-house.

Prior to the construction of King George's Gate in 1743, entrance to the town at this point had been through this open arch in the wall.

The last gate to be constructed in the old town pierced fortifications at the Southsea end of Pembroke Road. It was a plain structure known as King William IV Gate, having been erected in 1833-4 in lieu of a postern called the Spur Gate.

An original photograph of 1888 recorded after the removal of the gate, shows the moat and the town walls before they too were obliterated. The gatehouse seen on the left remains today though lacking its columned portal.

Of the several military engineers responsible for the design and construction of the town's defences, it was the Dutch military engineer Sir Bernard De Gomme who created the Camber Bastion, Long Curtain Moat, ramparts and Spur redoubt c.1670. The moat together with a small section beyond, and to the left of the wooden bridge, are all that remain of a system which once surrounded the town. The small bridge is a replacement of the original, across which, in 1805, Viscount Lord Nelson is said to have escaped the crowds of well wishers, to gain the beach and board the cutter which would take him to H.M.S. *Victory*, anchored at Spithead.

A reverse view of the previous photograph reveals, beyond the closed end of the moat, the narrow entrance to Portsmouth Harbour and the defences on the Gosport shore.

The massive fortified walls pictured, are those concealing the earlier Point Barracks and Eighteen Gun Battery in Broad Street. The spire and tower seen above the far wall are those surmounting Tower House, the one-time home of the marine artist W.L. Wyllie R.A.

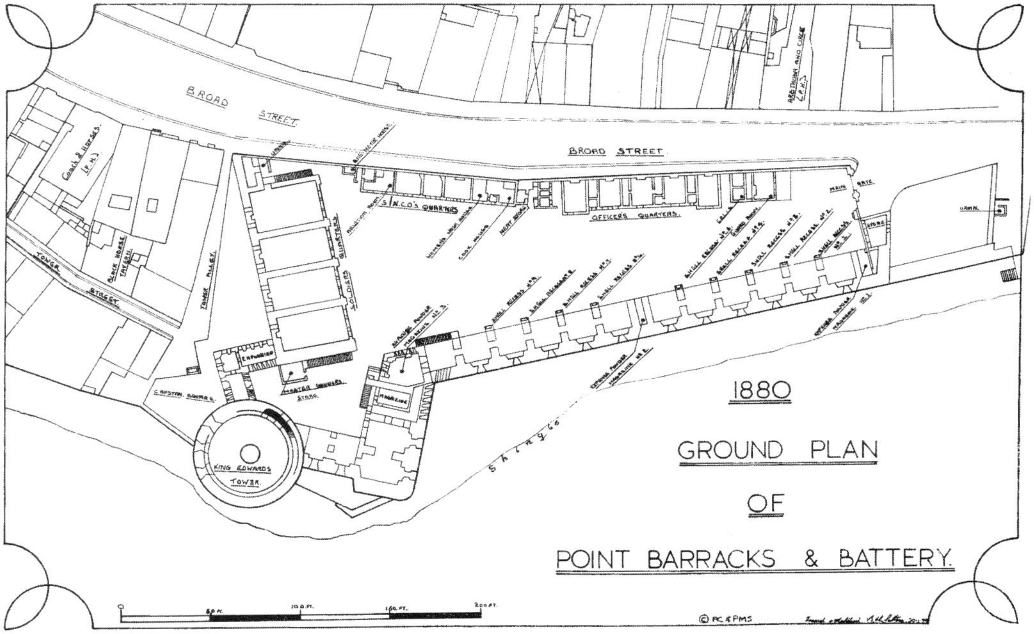

Point Battery (Barracks), Eighteen Gun Battery and the Round Tower are seen in this superb ground plan of c.1880, executed by Brian Patterson. The entire complex was purchased for the City of Portsmouth under an agreement with the War Office in 1958. The premises had a frontage of 500 feet to Broad Street and included the Round Tower and promenade on the seaward side. A sum of £8600 had been agreed for the site. With the subsequent removal of the barrack wall and the accompanying military accommodation, the site has since been open to the public.

The line of the wall was breached in two places to allow access to the small beach that is exposed at low tide. These two photographs show the most famous of the exits, the 'Sally Port', the departure point for so many of Britain's national heroes when embarking for foreign shores, adventures and battles. This was also the departure point for early emigrants to our colonies in the Americas and those miscreants being transported to Australia.

A little to the east of Sally Port, the defensive sea wall, continues to the Square Tower. This postcard view includes the Victoria Pier. Built in 1842, it was the first of the Portsmouth piers and provided, via the ferries, a link with the Isle of Wight.

Continuing in an easterly direction from the Pier and Square Tower, the unbroken defensive line is maintained by the Ten Gun Battery and the Saluting Battery Platform. The Saluting Battery, as the name implies, hosted the guns, which traditionally fired a salute to welcome members of the Royal Family and other visiting dignitaries. The guns were later sited further east on the Long Curtain Ramparts.

Royal and other traditional salutes are now fired from Blockhouse Fort in Gosport, there no longer being a military presence in Portsmouth. Before the practice ceased in Portsmouth however, the guns had been relocated from the old saluting battery to this position on the Ramparts overlooking the Garrison Church on the one side, and the Long Curtain Moat on the other. The tradition of firing an evening gun at sunset each day finally ceased in September 1931.

A superb aerial view encompassing almost all of the old town and recorded c.1934 shows in the foreground, the defensive wall supporting the Battery and Saluting Platform adjoining the Square Tower and Victoria Pier.

Beached against that very wall on September 4th 1909, is the paddle steamer *Duchess of Kent*, At 3.30pm on Friday 3rd, the vessel, on leaving the harbour and heading for Clarence Pier, was in collision with a collier, the *S.S. Transporter,* which was also leaving the harbour. The *Duchess of Kent* began to take in water and the captain immediately brought her ashore on to the narrow beach near Victoria Pier. The passengers, numbering approximately 400, were all brought safely ashore. After a swift temporary repair, the vessel, under its own steam, proceeded to Southampton on the following Sunday.

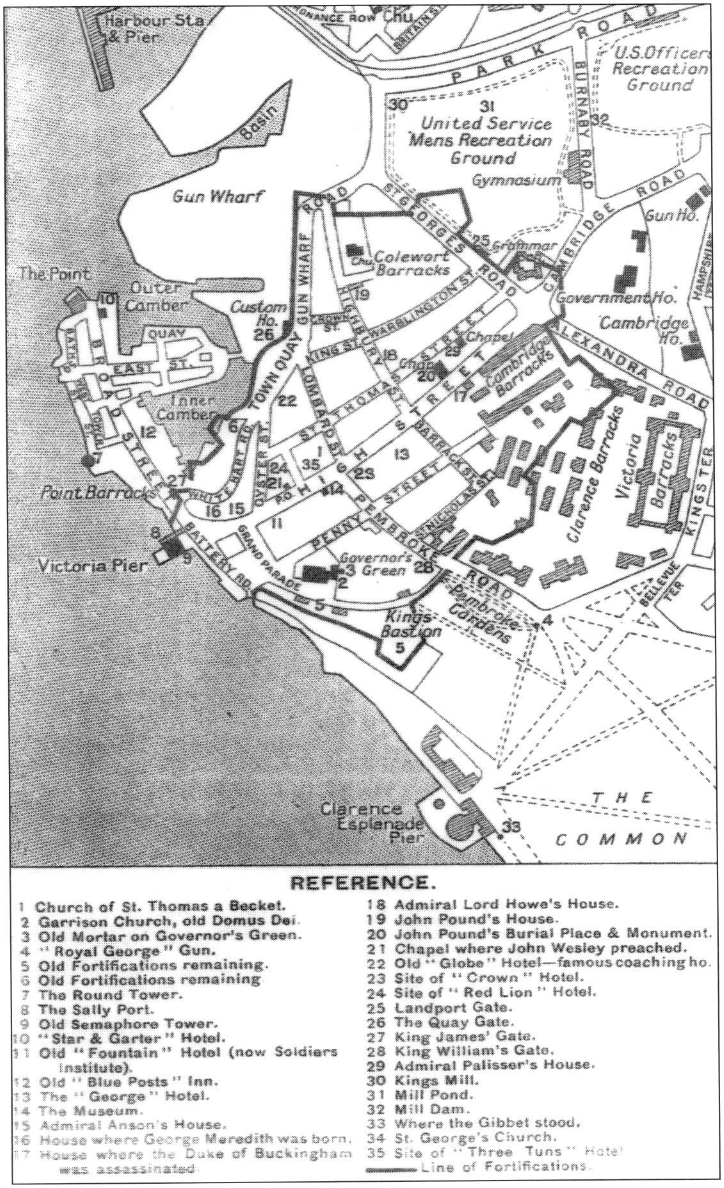

The Garrison Town of Portsmouth in 1860. Now even more heavily defended, it includes the four established barracks of Colewort, Cambridge, Clarence and Point, whilst just beyond the boundaries of the town are Milldam Barracks and the Gunwharf.

PORTSMOUTH AT PRAYER

The earliest known church to be established on Portsea Island was Saint Mary's, Portsea (Fratton) c.1170. The present building is on the site of two (possibly three) earlier such centres of worship. The early Saint Mary's would have served the needs of several hamlets on the island.

The community centred around the Camber and growing settlement of Old Portsmouth, however, had to wait just a little longer c.1180, before John De Gisors granted to the Canons of Southwick, 'for the repose of my soul and the souls of my father and mother and of my ancestors and my heirs, a certain place to erect thereon, a chapel in honour of the glorious Martyr, Thomas, Archbishop of Canterbury, on my land which is called Sudwede in the Isle of Portsia'. The chapel incidentally, became the first in Britain to be dedicated to the martyred saint. The illustration is believed to be the earliest known and is attributed to a date sometime in the sixteenth century.

In 1927, following the Borough of Portsmouth being elevated to 'City' status in 1926, Saint Thomas's became the Anglican Cathedral Church of the newly created Diocese of Portsmouth. The need to enlarge the old building and provide facilities to meet the demands of an appointed and enthroned bishop, meant that throughout the 1930s work continued to implement these improvements. With the declaration of war in September 1939, work was necessarily brought to a halt, leaving the newly constructed nave incomplete, against a temporary west wall.

Bombing during the war years accounted for the loss of approximately 50% of the old town. The view shows the bomb damage now cleared away and new buildings replacing those lost or damaged during the raids. The cruciform design of the original, tiny twelfth-century Saint Thomas's shows up well in this photograph c.1970.

Following the initial clearance of debris and several properties which had once fronted the High Street, the Cathedral was exposed to view. (It was only after the clearance that the Cathedral was considered to be in the High Street, the original address being St Thomas's Street.)

Surrounded by devastating bomb damage east, west, north and south, it is indeed a miracle that the Cathedral survived the war. This photograph is of White Hart Road and Oyster Street.

Courtesy of *The News* Portsmouth

Following the war, plans were revived to complete the abandoned extension of 1939 and this illustration is of the proposed new nave. The distinguished architect Lord Mottistone devised an entirely new treatment for the completion. 'The design being an expression of the century that witnessed the turning point in history, known simply as "D-Day". The completion of Portsmouth Cathedral as a memorial to D-Day together with a living recognition of the objectives of the subsequent victory, is an undertaking which we should be not only willing, but eager to enter into.'

The plans were eagerly accepted and agreed upon by the bishop, the Right Reverend John Phillips, and endorsed by Viscount Montgomery of Alamein, together with a great number of parishioners and citizens of Portsmouth. It was anticipated that the anniversary of D-Day 1969, would see the opening and dedication of the completed building. Financial restraints, however, caused the plans to be shelved and indeed later abandoned.

During the 1980s, further updated ideas were considered and accepted for yet another scheme to complete the building, this time from plans submitted by Michael Drury, a young architect from Salisbury who began work with elements of Nicholson's 1930s' design. In 1989, with an appeal target of £3 million, fund raising began in earnest and work to complete the nave was forecast for November 1991.

Plans of the proposed building works were heavily criticised by parishioners and townsfolk alike, the local press publishing numerous letters both for and against the design: 'Portsmouth's Parish Church since 1320, now takes on the appearance of a Turkish Fortress', was just one of the opinions voiced in the local press.

The now completed west-end of the Cathedral is pictured alongside the High Street and facing Oyster Street and, whatever the opinions and feelings voiced at the time, the mediaeval, Anglican Cathedral of St Thomas a Becket is the hub of the old town and remains, as it has done for almost 700 years, Portsmouth's Parish Church.

Eight of St Thomas's ten bells were originally cast in 1703 and were a gift from Admiral Sir George Rooke, then M.P. for Portsmouth. Persistent stories that they had once hung in Dover Castle and were a gift from Prince George of Denmark can be discounted, for the Dover bells remained there until 1779. This picture was taken in 1912, prior to a complete recasting. In 1957, a further two bells were added to the tower, so completing the present peal of ten. Tradition has it that the original bells were actually cast in a High Street foundry on a site later to be occupied by the George Hotel.

Above left: Late in the nineteenth century, the church was seen to be suffering from old age, and suspicions that all was not as it should be beneath the flooring, concerning particularly modern ideas of health and sanitation, proved to be well founded. Centuries of burials beneath the floor, the decaying state of coffins and their contents, gave rise to bad odours throughout the building, odours so acute that the Medical Officer of Health condemned the use of the church for public worship; the church was closed for two years whilst the floor was lifted, the offending remains removed and placed together in one long vault and repairs made to the north wall of the chancel which was visibly bulging inwards. The picture shows the beam and it's bracing, which was placed between the walls to temporarily arrest the imminent collapse of this section of the building.

Above right: Box pews were often a feature of old churches with parishioners buying or renting their right to what was sometimes a 'family' pew, or perhaps purchasing a moiety (part share) of a pew. The Church of St Thomas was predominantly furnished with such pews, each accessed via its own door. Now long since removed, these box pews are viewed from the west end c.1910. The supporting beam described in the previous photograph is seen in the distance.

Currently displayed within the Cathedral is the Golden Barque, originally placed on the cupola of the tower as a weather vane in 1710. During a storm in 1954, however, it came crashing to the ground and was almost destroyed on impact. Since its repair it has remained on display whilst a replica has taken its place on the Cathedral tower.

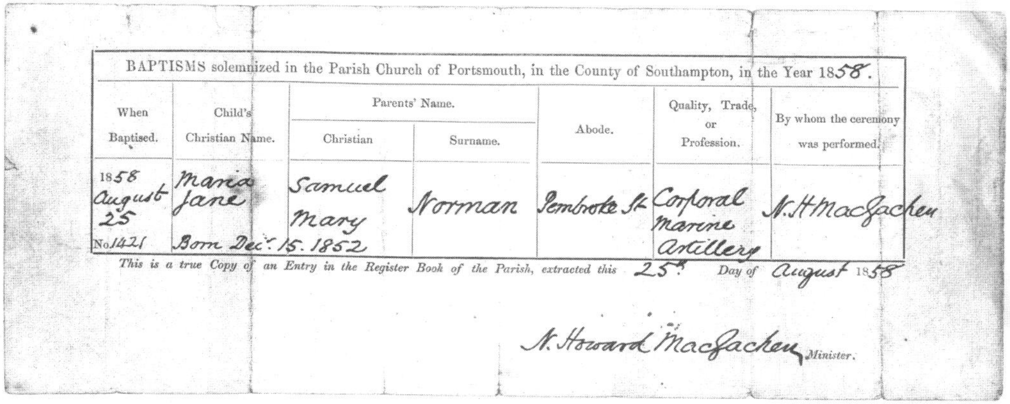

BAPTISMS solemnized in the Parish Church of Portsmouth, in the County of Southampton, in the Year 1858.

When Baptised.	Child's Christian Name.	Parents' Name. Christian	Parents' Name. Surname.	Abode.	Quality, Trade, or Profession.	By whom the ceremony was performed.
1858 August 25 No 1421	Maria Jane Born Decr. 15. 1852	Samuel Mary	Norman	Pembroke St.	Corporal Marine Artillery	N. H. MacGachen

This is a true Copy of an Entry in the Register Book of the Parish, extracted this 25th Day of August 1858

N. Howard MacGachen Minister.

Dated 1858, a valued document from the family archive is this certificate recording the baptism at the Church of Saint Thomas, of Maria Jane Norman, Great, Great Grandmother of the author. Note that the parental home was at Pembroke Street (now Pembroke Road), Old Portsmouth.

Throughout the 19th century, a continued increase in the population of 'Greater Portsmouth' (Portsea Island) also witnessed an increase in the number of chapel and church buildings erected. Old Portsmouth was no exception and in 1839 a Chapel of Ease, the Church of Saint Mary, Portsmouth (not to be confused with Saint Mary Portsea), was consecrated in Colewort Garden Street (later to be named Saint Mary's Street, White Horse Street and later still, Highbury Street). Having a relatively short life, the church was demolished in 1921. The architect here was Thomas Ellis Owen, who also designed the church of Saint Mary Portsea in 1843.

Occupying a site immediately next door to garage premises in High Street, the Portsmouth Unitarian Chapel could boast origins from 1718 when it started life as a Presbyterian place of worship. Another casualty of the war years when thirty city churches and chapels were destroyed or badly damaged, the chapel has since been rebuilt, the foundation stone being laid by Sir Adrian Boult on 24 September 1955. Adopting the additional title of St John Pounds Memorial Church, the reader will turn to the later references to John Pounds.

The oblique camera angle of this photograph is intentional for, whilst it shows the present post-war Unitarian Chapel, it also includes the next door property which is unique in that it is clad with 'mathematical' tiles; the only known example in Portsmouth. This rare type of wall facing has a brick-sized 'face' header or stretcher and a recessed flange above with one or more fixing holes. The tiles are placed to cover the wall until the overall appearance is that of a brick surface with mortar pointing, to complete the illusion.

The tiles have been so named 'mathematical' since before 1830; so far, there has been no explanation as to why; suffice to say that there are 800 examples known, all but one being in England. The nearby town of Havant also has just one building partially clad in this way.

The Royal Garrison Church, seriously damaged by the bombing in the Second World War, is now all that remains of the ancient hospital (hospice) founded c.1212 by Peter de Rupibus, Bishop of Winchester. With the hospital dedicated to Saint Nicholas and its chapel to Saint John the Baptist, the building adopted the title of Domus Dei (God's House).

In the mid sixteenth century it was taken over by the state and for twenty years at least, became an armoury for the garrison. Having served as hospital, chapel and armoury, the chapel was later to be joined by apartments including the Governor's Residence. It was in the Presence Chamber of the Governor's House that King Charles II married Catherine of Braganza in 1662. The house and adjoining buildings were demolished in 1826.

The graveyard of the Royal Garrison Church contains this fine memorial to General Sir James Charles Napier. A most gallant and popular soldier, he died at his home, 'Oaklands' at Waterlooville, and was laid to rest on 8 September 1853. The route, along which the cortege made its way to the church, was lined with a crowd estimated at 50,000, in addition to 3000 uniformed men of the garrison who were intent on paying homage and respect to a heroic general. It is thought unlikely that the tomb pictured contains or covers his remains; he probably lies in a vaulted grave beneath the floor of the nave.

Recorded in 1888, the photograph is of a memorial to those members of The King's Regiment who lost their lives in the Indian Mutiny 1857/59. Once a feature of the Grand Parade, the memorial has since been relocated to the City of Liverpool.

Often referred to as the Cathedral of the British Army, the Royal Garrison Church is pictured at a date sometime in the 1930s; colours of various regiments display battle honours gained in military campaigns throughout the world.

Sunday Church Parades were guaranteed to attract large crowds who would gather to witness the traditional spectacle of military bands and marching troops. Spectators surround the Grand Parade Ground whilst the nearby raised Saluting Platform, provides a grandstand view.

A number of military barracks were located in Old Portsmouth at no great distance from the church. Here, the band of the Royal Artillery leads a column of troops through Penny Street *en route* to a traditional Sunday Church Parade.

A final glimpse of the troops parading before an appreciative public prior to a short march back to barracks in 1934.

BROAD STREET AND PORTSMOUTH POINT

With the Square Tower on the left of the picture, the view is of the entrance to a pre-war Broad Street which, until the bombing, had provided the visitor with a real flavour of Old Portsmouth. The family group are admiring the gilded bust of Charles I, which has occupied a decorative niche in the upper wall since 1635.

The overhead tram wires suggest an earlier date than that of the previous picture; the scene however, is again of Broad Street, this time at a different location. Whilst most of the left-hand buildings remain undamaged, those on the right were totally destroyed during air raids on the City.

A most unusual feature still to be seen in Broad Street is the archway that once afforded access to Capstan House, the studio premises of W.H.Wyllie R.A. the well-known marine artist. The building itself was destroyed in the blitz but the decorative arch remains; its unique incised inscription, 'Lat.30-47-25 North. Long. 1-6-25.West' proclaims its actual position in the world! The fifteenth-century Round Tower is also seen in the photograph.

Capstan House, is on the corner of Tower Alley, which in times past led from Broad Street to Capstan Square. Legend has it that the substantial timber wall on the left-hand side of the alley was constructed by William Wyllie from timbers purchased from local ship breakers, they being identical to 'tween deck stanchions in old ships of war.

The Round Tower, guardian of the entrance to Portsmouth Harbour since c.1418, shares the photograph with Tower House, the home of William Wyllie. The tower and spire topping the house, were added in the years following the First World War.

The engraving is of Capstan Square in the eighteenth century, again with the Round Tower included. It was here in 1522 that a capstan was installed to raise a 'mighty chain' across the entrance to the harbour 'from Point to Blockhouse' on the Gosport shore. The chain was designed to lie on the seabed and in the event of a French raid on the town, to be raised to the surface supported by lighters, so blocking the harbour mouth. It is thought unlikely that it was ever called upon to be used in such an emergency.

The Blue Posts in Broad Street was one of the great inns of the old town. It dated from c.1613, and until the coming of the railway was one of the principle coaching inns. The original building was destroyed by fire on 7 May 1870. This picture shows its replacement, though lacking the blue painted portal columns from which the name was derived. Bombing during the blitz of 1941 destroyed this building.

Portsmouth is often referred to as the Birthplace of Australia, 28,000 felons and their guards having set sail from here. Of that number, very few would see England again. In 1980, Australia's bi-centennial year was celebrated both here and in Sydney and monuments erected as a tangible expression of bonds uniting the two cities and dedicated to thousands of settlers who built the nation of Australia. The Portsmouth monument, standing near the Sally Port from where thousands of settlers took their last steps on British soil, is dull and tarnished to represent the old country, while the monument in Sydney, standing on the spot where Captain Arthur Phillip first raised the flag, is bright and shiny signifying the new country.

Portsmouth's monument stands on a plinth of granite from New South Wales, whereas the Sydney monument stands on a base of granite from England.

Another more recent addition to Broad Street is a statue erected in September 2001, dedicated to those Mormon idealists who, placing their lives in the hands of God set out to discover a promised land and new life in America. The 7ft bronze effigy depicts a couple with two small children preparing to depart these shores on what will be a perilous journey. The casemates of the old Point Barracks provide the background.

Backing on to the Camber Basin, this fine pair of Georgian houses bearing the name 'Dore Court', is sited on the east side of Broad Street. With the addition of penthouse rooms and a shared balcony, the properties enjoy unsurpassed views of Spithead, the Solent and passing shipping.

Recorded sometime before 1911, Number 39 Broad Street was the premises of Loader's Temperance Dining Rooms, serving meals such as mother would make!

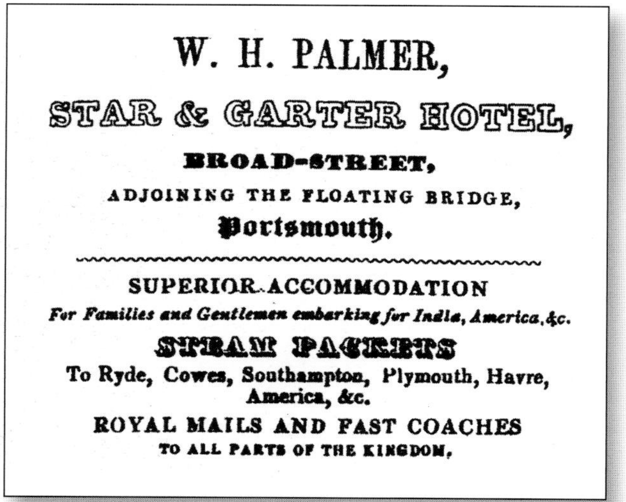

An advertisement for the Hotel dated 1841, perhaps suggests that passengers bound for India, America etc. would sail from Portsmouth?

Courtesy of Anthony Triggs

A scheme to improve facilities at the Camber was submitted to the council in September 1956. It involved the removal of all properties between East Street and the Star and Garter Hotel on the east side of Broad Street to provide car parking space and a new berth for the Isle of Wight car ferry.

Dating from the mid sixteenth century, the Hotel was removed in what has since been considered an act of civic vandalism, particularly as the ferry has since been relocated to yet another berth.

Courtesy of Anthony Triggs

The pictured demolition is a sad reminder of a once popular, famous and historic hotel, that had in its day accommodated such noted persons as Lord Nelson, Lord Howe and Sir John and Lady Franklin. The picture also reveals how close the building was to the waterside of Portsmouth Harbour.

Heading a detachment of troops, the Duke of Connaught is making his way to the chain ferry which will take them to Browndown Ranges in Gosport, where they are to take part in a military exercise. The date, 28 August 1894.

Soldiers of the Royal Horse Artillery together with horses, field guns and limbers, form an orderly queue on the nearside of Broad Street whilst waiting their turn to board the ferry.

The military exercise over, the Royal Horse Artillery returns from Gosport...

...followed by a detachment of the Royal Marine Artillery.

With the Gosport and Isle of Wight ferries no longer operating from Point, the access ramps have been removed and the seaward end of Broad Street raised above the old beach level. In times past, however, the periodic and seasonal flooding of the street had to be endured; most of the properties seen, had boards always at the ready to slot in place to stop the ingress of sea-water through the front doors.

This view confirms the fact that traffic waiting to board the Portsmouth to Gosport chain ferry, queued on the 'nearside of the street.

A further two views of the flooded street reveal that the photographic chemist, Herbert H. Bailey, (c.1911) has taken over the business premises of the late W.B. Townley. The advertising lantern provides the clue! Note the spectators in the upstairs windows.

Continuing with the theme of the ferry services, Broad Street was the embarkation point for three distinct enterprises and most readers will be surprised to learn that, prior to the bombing sustained during the Second World War, a passenger ferry service was provided between Old Portsmouth and Gosport. The picture shows the vessel at its berth between the ramp (left) of the Isle of Wight car ferry and (right) the ramp for the chain ferry to Gosport.

The local tramway terminated at Point for the convenience of intending boat passengers while a horse-drawn fleet of vehicles awaits a harbour crossing to Gosport.

Before the introduction of steam and motor vessels, the only method of transporting horses and cattle to the Isle of Wight was the 'tow boat'; as the name implies, small tugboats towed these craft.

Vehicles from the Isle of Wight disembark from the car ferry whilst a motley collection queues for a crossing of the Solent.

The increasing popularity of the motorcar, gave yet more business to the tow boats that readily carried vehicles to, and from, the Island.

A novel and alternative use was to provide a setting for this group of happy children to pose for a photograph.

It was 1927 before the Southern Railway Company introduced the first of the purpose-built car ferries to serve on the Point to Fishbourne route. The vessel pictured is the *Wootton*.

An innovative chain-operated 'Floating Bridge' was introduced to the harbour scene as long ago as 1840 and provided a vital link between Gosport and Portsmouth. The last of its three vessels was constructed in 1864 and continued in service until 1959 when the service ceased.

This unusual view shows the floating bridge approaching the Portsmouth shore, the tension of its chain mechanism being governed by a large weight rising and falling within a 'well-like' shaft on shore.

Long before the establishment of a purpose-built fish market in Portsmouth, local catches were sold, usually by auction, in front of the Still and West and, like the great London markets, special dispensation was granted allowing the pub to open from four o'clock in the morning.

Passengers awaiting either of the three local ferry services could perhaps avail themselves of the hospitality of three adjacent public houses, the Still and West Country House being just one of them, the alternatives being, the Union Tavern and the Coal Exchange.

Recorded in 1973, the scene changes to one of a leisure pursuit; folk can sit, relax and enjoy the ever-changing panorama of Portsmouth Harbour.

Quebec House; a timber-framed building in Bath Square (or Bathing House Square), was built by public subscription as a bathing house in 1754, when an early guide says, 'in this Bathing House are likewise hot baths and two good dressing-rooms, one for the ladies, the other for gentlemen, and every other necessary commodity'. There were four baths of different depths of water, two of them deep enough to swim in. In the nineteenth century it became part of the then adjacent Quebec Hotel, and has retained the name. The Quebec Hotel was also memorable as the place where Captain Seton was taken after being mortally wounded in a duel of 1845, when he had been refused admission to the Royal Naval Hospital at Haslar. Constructed entirely of timber and clad in weatherboarding it is of a style now unique in Portsmouth.

Photographed on 16 January 1907, the scene is once more of Portsmouth Point at the start of a 1700 mile marathon 'trundle' undertaken by local blacksmith Mr W.Hayes. Hayes earlier accepted a challenge to 'trundle' (hand propel) a pair of cartwheels north to Newcastle and Carlisle, returning to Portsmouth via Penzance and Plymouth in 100 days. Afterwards known as the 'Human Axle', he exceeded all expectations by completing the marathon journey in 97 days!

It is said that he passed through every county in England with the exception of Wiltshire. His trainer Mr Elliot and a referee who was there to see fair play accompanied him throughout; the challenge, after all, involved Mr Hayes receiving £500 from the challenger who had foolishly bet that such a feat would be an impossibility.

Dated 1831, the plan of the Island of Portsea by J. Maynard shows the old town of Portsmouth to be overshadowed by the neighbouring 'new' town of Portsea and the growing districts of Landport and Southsea. It will be noticed that at this time, both Portsmouth and Portsea are still heavily defended and will remain so until the late1860s and early '70s.

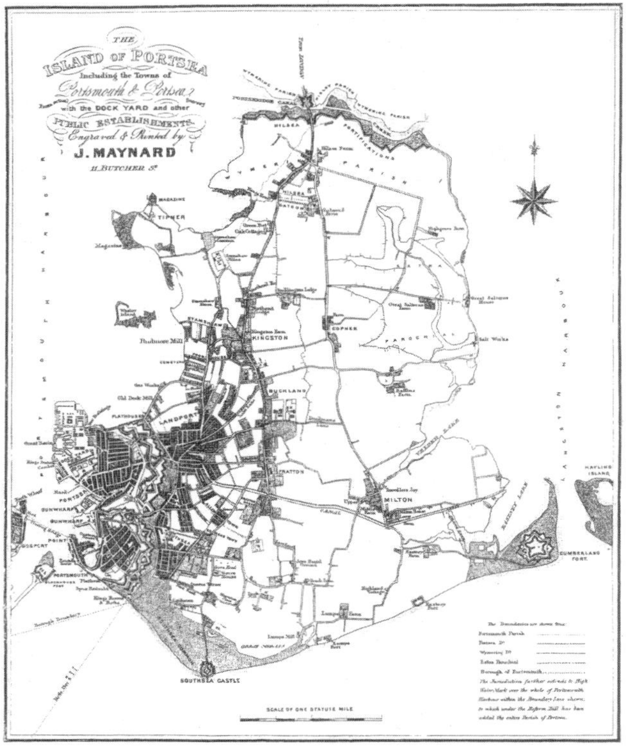

PORTSMOUTH HIGH STREET

This view is of the second Portsmouth Grammar School building; it opened in 1879, following a move from its original home in Penny Street where the school had been founded by Dr William Smith in 1732. The building pictured, is located facing, though not actually in, High Street. It is, therefore, within just a few yards of being within the boundaries of the old town.

The new, and present buildings housing the Grammar School had earlier been the Cambridge Barracks and were purchased from the War Office in 1926 for £10,000. To convert the premises, a further £13,000 was needed so, an appeal was launched by the Mayor, Councillor Frank J. Privett, whose own generous contribution amounted to £7500.

The George Hotel, famous for its association with Lord Nelson, is where the Admiral had breakfast and spent his final hours ashore before leaving for his last, and greatest, battle at Trafalgar. Sadly the hotel was destroyed during the air raids on Portsmouth.

A short distance from the barracks is Buckingham House where, on 23 August 1628, John Felton, who was aggrieved at being passed over for promotion, murdered the Duke of Buckingham. The Duke, whilst a favourite of King Charles I 'who loved and trusted him above all others', was the most hated man in England. Generally disliked by the soldiers and sailors who had earlier demonstrated about non-payment of their wages, he was, said one member of the House of Commons, 'the cause of all our miseries; the Duke of Buckingham, is the grievance of all our grievances'.

The Theatre Royal in the High Street is reproduced from an engraved aquatint by T. Woodfall 1803. Built in 1761, the theatre was demolished in 1854 following its acquisition by the War Office who then constructed Cambridge Barracks (the present Grammar School) in its place.

The building with nine or so uniformed men standing in front was, in its final years, the Portsmouth branch of the Y.M.C.A; at the time of this photograph however, it is the Portsmouth Soldiers Institute founded by Miss Sarah Robinson.

Lord Nelson was idolised as a hero in his own lifetime, so to avoid the crowd of admirers and well wishers who had gathered outside the hotel at the time of his departure, he is said to have slipped out via the yard and rear exit in Penny Street, before making for the shore and the boat which would convey him to H.M.S. *Victory*.

Yet another building lost to the town during the blitz, was the City Museum. Opened as the New Town Hall in 1838, it had replaced the Old Town Hall that, together with its market and 'shambles', had occupied an inconvenient site in the centre of the High Street.

Sarah Robinson (1834-1921), sought to spread Christian standards of morals and behaviour among soldiers. She began her work in Aldershot, visiting barracks and brothels and encouraging temperance activities. She established a permanent Soldiers Institute at the Old Fountain Inn in Portsmouth's High Street in 1874, where accommodation and other facilities were provided for soldiers, sailors and their wives. The Fountain Inn had earlier been the town house of Sir John Suffield, who also had a country residence at Widley Manor House in the one-time hamlet north of Portsdown Hill.

The High Street Institute (picture from the rear, in Penny Street) was just one of several such establishments, which Miss Robinson created in Portsmouth, others being located in Nobb's Lane and the Welcome Institute in Stanhope Road. This High Street building was demolished in 1970.

The success of Miss Robinson's campaign was acknowledged when hard-living men accepted a Christian/Temperance way of life as a result of attending lectures and Bible classes. In this photograph of 1876, a class comprises Royal Marines and one sailor.

Sarah Robinson's Helping Hand and Temperance Society welcomed wives of servicemen into its civilian branch and, on this very colourful, decorative certificate of membership, it will be noted that Mrs Maria Rimmington (the same Maria (Norman) whose Baptism certificate appears earlier in this volume), has been admitted into the society, having 'signed the pledge' in 1885.

The officer classes were later included in Miss Robinson's plans and, as finance became available, premises were leased or purchased to extend her good works. The buildings pictured are located in Penny Street and Grand Parade.

A cripple from birth, Miss Robinson was, nevertheless, a keen traveller, and for most of her life had to be transported in a variety of early 'hospital type' carriages devoid of any comfort including such basic refinements as sprung chassis or road springs (her own descriptions!). Having planned a one thousand mile tour of Britain in June 1889, she had this ambulance coach built to order which boasted springs and rubber tyres in addition to a sprung bed, lockers and ample space. She is pictured (the small figure in the left hand window) with her friend and sole companion Alice Halls, prior to setting off on her latest adventure.

Her departure from Penny Street at the rear of the High Street premises, is witnessed by her Institute Supervisor Mr Tufnell, Mr Reading the coach builder and members of the Institute staff.

Horse trams were introduced into the old town in 1874, terminating at Point via High Street. Horse-drawn vehicles were replaced by electric tramcars between 1901 and 1903. This scene was probably recorded shortly following the introduction of the service in 1874.

Right: Pictured is number 74 High Street, one-time residence of Admiral Anson, First Lord of the Admiralty in 1751 and Admiral of the Fleet in 1761. A study of the previous picture reveals his home to have been converted to business premises (opticians) in the later, Victorian period. In company with much of the High Street, the house was destroyed in the bombing raids.

Far right: The present public house The Duke of Buckingham is a post-war rebuild bearing no resemblance to this, the pre-war premises. Both the current and previous hostelries occupy the same location on the corner of Highbury Street and High Street and take their name from the late Duke who was murdered in 1628 in a house (see earlier reference in this section) across the road.

The High Street Post Office was opened in 1858, following the closure of the Portsmouth Office in Pembroke Street. It was considered to be adequate for the entire Borough and, for many years, it was the General Post Office for the town until the opening of the new Landport General Post Office in Commercial Road in 1883. The High Street Office was also destroyed in the war.

POSTWAR ARCHAEOLOGY

Courtesy of Portmouth City Museums and Records Services

The major destruction of Old Portsmouth during the Second World War and the subsequent clearance of the debris, exposed large tracts of land ripe for archaeological exploration. It was not until 1968, however, that funding and expertise became available to allow work to commence; although it was not always possible or practical to probe each and every bombed site in the town, it was thought necessary to determine whether or not evidence of our ancient past and ancestry lay beneath what was considered to be the oldest and therefore the most interesting sites. The area adjacent to the Camber Dock became the first to be worked upon.

An aerial view of the site shows just how close the 'dig' site (highlighted) was to the edge of the Camber Dock wall; the reader is asked to imagine a situation where, before any land reclamation, the natural shoreline offered the only means of berthing or loading a vessel. 'Camber' originally meant a small dock where cambering (the bending and shaping of ships timbers) was carried out.

Photo Courtesy of *The News* - Portsmouth

Above left: Early drawings show the natural lagoon that was to become the Camber, to have been much larger than today. The construction of quays, associated warehousing, together with docking, ship building and massive coal handling facilities, have seen a reduction in the actual water area. Suffice to say, that archaeology has revealed an original shoreline including (primitive, by today's standards) the timber remains of a fourteenth/fiteenth century purpose-built dock with later retaining walls some little distance inland from the present water's edge, beyond White Hart Road and bordering the actual dig site. **Above right:** Anglesea Court, Oyster Street, which lay within a triangle of land formed by Lombard Street, Highbury Street and White Hart Road, became available for examination in July 1969. The site did indeed, realise the expectations of the archaeology team, proving to be rich with evidence of earlier, perhaps seasonal habitation, including worked flint from the Neolithic to the Bronze Age, 2500-1500 B.C. The discovery of numerous freshwater springs and wells gave further evidence of an inducement for our ancestors to create a settlement here (almost certainly the earliest on Portsea Island).

These buildings are the only examples which remained on site throughout the period of excavation and are of uncertain age, the older possibly dating from as early as the twelfth century. The other, once a store, has since been tastefully transformed into a dwelling house, bearing the name 'Popinjay's; a sixteenth-century map shows two properties in Oyster Street with that name, one a house, the other a warehouse.

Above left: Grand Parade, viewed and researched as a location of especial archaeological interest. that is, the actual military parade area adjacent to the Royal Garrison Church. Work began in 1972, in the expectation that remains of sixteenth-century buildings associated with both the church and Governor's residence would be discovered. With the turf removed, a considerable area of hard-packed stone, flint, pebbles etc was revealed, suggestive perhaps of an earlier parade ground for military assemblies. **Above right:** Continuing with the general excavation of the Grand Parade site in October 1972, a mystery tunnel, probably of Tudor origin, was discovered. Located between the Royal Garrison Church and the Long Curtain ramparts, it happened to be a 'chance find' when the team were hoping to discover the site, or evidence, of the remains of Bishop Moleyn's Chapel built after 1449. The chapel was built by the people of Portsmouth as a penance for the murder of the bishop by rioting seamen. Following the murder, the whole of Portsmouth was excommunicated. A trial excavation revealed stone that was originally thought to be part of the chapel wall. The tunnel was uncovered during the digging operations. Constructed of stones with a corbelled roof, it appears to have been a link between the old Governor's House and the sea and/or the Square Tower.

Right: A study of immediate soil samples, provided clues as to what perhaps may lie beneath the surface and, indeed, this photograph of a slightly later date, revealed positive evidence of earlier buildings.

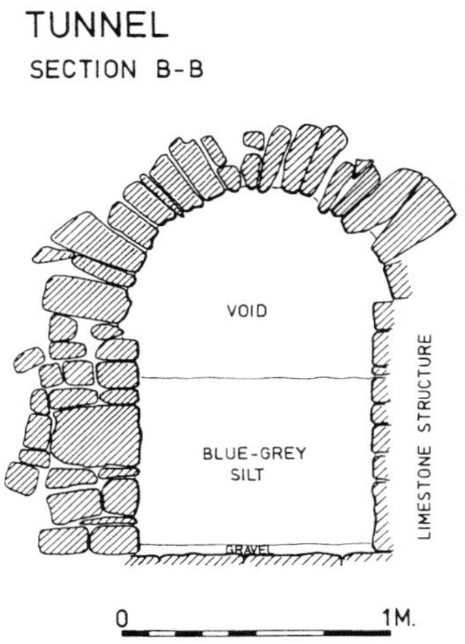

Left: The drawing of the tunnel, produced by archaeologist Russell T. Fox, shows that the dimensions would have certainly allowed the passage of men, albeit perhaps stooping a little. The tunnel has since been covered once again and remains an unsolved enigma within the City. English Heritage, custodians of the land, will not permit any future disturbance or evaluation of the plot.

Below left: Removal of the grass and soil revealed a well-constructed entrance of 'fortress' proportions.

Advancing further, the archaeological team found that a short central passage gave access to a number of rooms, each hinting at a one-time military installation reminiscent perhaps of the nineteenth century Palmerston Forts. Yet one more surprising discovery disclosed that whilst there was now no powered connection to the building, there had been at some time long ago a system of electric lighting throughout!

A rare photograph of the De Gomme ramparts of 1665, revised in 1730, and altered yet again with the addition of the brick building let into the rampart itself. It is not known exactly when, or for what reason, this additional feature was installed or when its use was discontinued, for no external trace now remains. In 1974, however, a decision was made to explore and fully examine this section of the rampart.

Preparations for a French attack during the Napoleonic Wars involved a continual update of the town's defences including those of the Long Curtain ramparts. An engraving from the *Illustrated London News* of 4 July 1846 shows the additions made to reinforce the original De Gomme ramparts. Now buried beneath grass and soil and part of the complete line of an earthen bank, they are seen constructed as individual units.

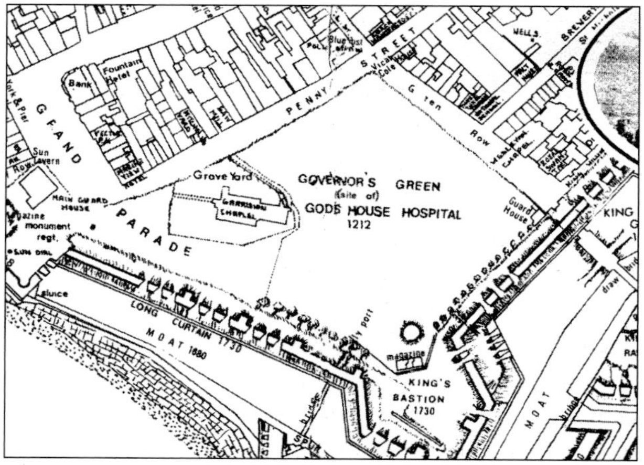

That the individual units are part of a continuous line is confirmed by referring to the drawing and noting the lower section backing on to the Long Curtain Moat.

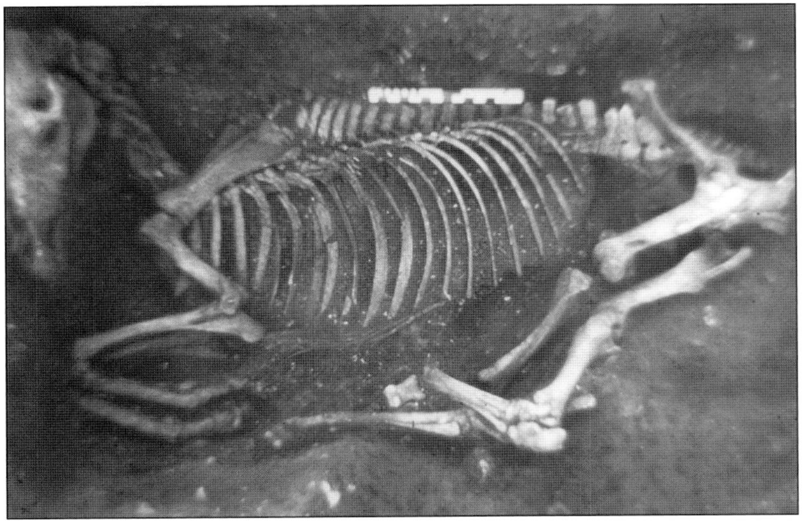

The most surprising and unexpected find was the complete skeleton of a horse buried in what had been the garden or grounds of the High St residence of the Military Govenor of the town. Bearing in mind that the Royal Naval Commander-in-Chief and the Town Governor had once dwelt here, it is likely that the horse had been a much loved and valued equine companion to one or other of the gentlemen.

A final look at the activities of our local archaeologists (in this volume at least) must include a situation perhaps forced upon them when, in October 1987, hurricane-force winds together with high tides, wrought havoc along Britain's south coast. Portsmouth's centuries-old defensive walls, having faced the elements since at least the sixteenth century were finally breached, not by an enemy but by nature herself. The original Tudor wall was exposed following the collapse of the eighteenth century reinforcing wall of the Saluting Battery.

JOHN POUNDS
Cobbler, Schoolmaster and Philanthropist

Founder of the Ragged School Movement, John Pounds was born in Portsmouth in 1766. At the age of fifteen years whilst employed in the dockyard, he suffered a crippling accident severely smashing his thighbone when he fell from a ship into a dry dock. Incapacitated and no longer employable, he set about the task of rebuilding his life and developed the skill of shoe making. His tiny dwelling, remembered by so many later Portsmouth folk, consisted of two rooms only; the lower his workshop and the upper, his scanty accommodation.

It was in these surroundings that whilst working, he also instilled into the local ragged street urchins, the rudiments of his own poor education. For those children who hungered for food as well as knowledge, he shared what food he had with them. The hundreds who attended his school-cum-workshop and followed his teaching until the day he died on 1 January 1839, are a measure of his success and influence among the children. He died still a poor man, poor that is in monetary terms but wealthy in that his example later brought about the worldwide Ragged School Movement.

Top left: John Pounds' house in St Mary's Street (later to be renamed Highbury Street) became, until its near destruction by enemy bombing during the war years, a Mecca for numbers of children who, having been told the story of the man and his good works, then often made school visits to view the actual house. This delightful photograph is of the Edwardian period. The author recalls his own school visit in the mid-1930s.

Top middle: A commercial picture postcard features the house in 1911.

Top right: It has been repeatedly claimed that the house, then in need of repair and restoration, was dismantled and placed into secure storage, awaiting attention and remedial work some time during 1939.This photograph is in itself, a denial of that claim. Much of Old Portsmouth was destroyed during a daylight raid on 12 August 1940, and this scene was recorded a short time after the event; proof indeed that the house had not been removed in 1939. The City of Portsmouth Records Series 1946 to 1955, page 282, states that the house and workshop were cleared away with surrounding derelict property during the Second World War to allow for extensions to the power station.

On 22 February 1954, The Lord Mayor of Portsmouth, Councillor G.A.Day, preserved the memory of John Pounds by unveiling a plaque at a site upon which had stood the humble home and workshop of this famous cobbler and educational pioneer among poor children, more than 100 years before. The plaque was placed on an extension to the power station which itself has since been demolished.

The late emeritus Minister of the Unitarian Church (John Pounds' Memorial Church) in the High Street, John Sturgess, enjoyed a fifty-year association with the church and nourished a dream that one day there should be a re-creation of John Pounds' house within the tiny churchyard. Sadly the Rev. Sturgess passed on before his dream was realised. However, a tribute to the two Johns, Pounds and Sturgess, is now complete and this imaginative replica of the original house, with resident mannequin figures, occupies a corner of the churchyard. Visitors to the church and graveyard, would do well to stop and note the dual epitaph inscribed on the monument above the grave of John Pounds, for who among us today could command a genuine and heartfelt dedication such as described on the two faces of the memorial?

Underneath this monument
Rest the mortal remains of
JOHN POUNDS
The Philanthropic Shoemaker
Of St. Mary's Street Portsmouth
Who while
Working at his trade in a very
Small room gratuitously
Instructed in useful education
And partly clothed and fed
Some hundreds of girls and boys
He died suddenly
On New Years Day MDCCCXXXIX
While in his active beneficence
Aged LXXII
Well done thou good and faithful
Servant, enter thou into the joy
of thy Lord
Verily I say unto thee in as much as
Thou hast done it unto one of the
Least of these my brethren thou
Hast done it unto me

This Monument
has been erected chiefly
By means of penny subscriptions
Not only from the Christian
Brotherhood
With whom John Pounds
Habitually worshipped
in the adjoining Chapel
but from persons of widely
differing religious opinion
throughout Great Britain
and from the most distant parts
of the World
In connection with this monument
Has also been founded in like manner
within these precincts
A LIBRARY TO HIS MEMORY
designed to extend
To an indefinite futurity
The solid mental and moral usefulness
To which the philanthropic shoemaker
Was so earnestly devoted
To the last days of his life
Pray for the Blessing of God to prosper it

PORTSMOUTH – POT POURRI

A Miscellaneous Selection of Illustrations and Comments

Recorded in February 1971, the view is of properties numbered 15 to 17 Lombard Street. In the background it is of interest to note the changes that have taken place on the Town Quay and the outer Camber. The Bridge Tavern, which today stands alone upon the quayside, is lost amid a mass of warehousing and stores.

Remaining briefly with the Bridge Tavern, this spectacular reproduction of the painting 'Portsmouth Point' by Thomas Rowlandson, now adorns almost an entire outside wall. The painting conveys Rowlandson's impression of the roistering and carousing which, so legend tells us, commonly took place on late seventeenth century Point.

Returning to Lombard Street. At its junction with St Thomas's Street, is an attractive group of houses featuring double-curved Dutch gables, probably dating from the middle of the seventeenth century. Behind the façades they may indeed be older and possibly timber framed. The corner property, now strikingly renamed 'Many Cargoes', was in the years 1932/34 the Youth Hostel Association's Portsmouth Hostel for females; males, meanwhile, were accommodated under a special arrangement with the Y.M.C.A. in their High Street premises.

Properties that fortunately survived the war years include Number 3 Penny Street, which in 1971 is seen enjoying a 'make-over'. Probably Georgian in origin, it is at the junction of Penny Street and the quaintly named Peacock Lane which was, more fittingly for its time, previously called Barrack Street. Penny Street is better known perhaps for the infamous town gaol once sited here.

Know locally as a Garrison House, this sixteenth-century example is pictured on the corner of St Thomas's and Highbury Streets. It was once forbidden to build houses higher than the town's defensive walls, thus creating a situation where the town was invariably enveloped in a confined and low-lying blanket of smoke, smog and putrid air.

White Hart Road is still to be found in the old town, although in the year 2006 it is unrecognisable from this photograph c.1935. The overhead coal transporter feeding the power station is seen in the distance.

This photograph of Oyster Street was recorded in the mid 1930s. Possibly the oldest inhabited part of the town, its origins date from at least the twelfth century.

Left: The Garage and Workshops of the United Service Garage, sited in the High Street, could also be accessed from nearby St Thomas's Street from where this picture was taken; an attractive display of 1928 vintage motorcars complements the scene. The building next door was, at this time, Smither's Pickle Factory.

Right: Fortunately escaping the blitz, it is not known exactly when the Royal Naval Club was built. It is known, however, that architect Thomas Hellyer designed the tower that was added in 1871. Legend has it that the tower was built so that a naval signalman stationed there, could receive and interpret flagged messages from vessels lying at Spithead, indicating that accommodation should be prepared for Naval Officers who would shortly be coming ashore.

Left: Pembroke Road pictured in 1911, has previously had a variety of names, the earliest being Genmell Street, then, in no particular order, Fighting Cocks Lane, Little Penny Lane, Pembroke Street and finally Pembroke Road; from Governors Green eastwards, however, it was known as Green Road. From right to left, the buildings at this time were, the Wesleyan Chapel, Whites Dining Rooms, The Royal Naval Club, Cole and Sons Gun Makers and Pembroke House.

In the latter half of the eighteenth century, Admiral Lord Howe resided here at Curzon House, Highbury Street. Sadly, this imposing property (later known as Highbury House) was yet another victim of the war years.

Clarence Barracks, built in 1880 as part of three military barrack units (the other two being Victoria and Cambridge), was certainly the most impressive of the three. (The photograph is of the south-facing, rear of the building.) Comments at the time acknowledged them to be 'the most palatial and finest barracks in every respect, erected in any part of the kingdom'. The three barracks were built on, or over, the old moats, ramparts and defences after they had been filled in and dismantled. In July 1970, Portsmouth City Council outlined plans to take over Clarence Barracks and, after limited alterations and sympathetic conversion, the building became the city's principal museum and art gallery.

A general view of all three barracks is portrayed on a postcard dated 1910.

Victoria Barracks, pictured here, served the Royal Navy as a shore establishment in its final years, before closing its gates for good on 29 August 1956.

King James's Gate was removed at the close of the nineteenth century to allow for road widening, together with the introduction of double-deck tramcars not being able to pass beneath the centre arch. The gate was then relocated, minus at least some of its original furnishings, to a site on the corner of St Michael's Road facing Hampshire Terrace from where this photograph was taken. The saga of the gate continued when the site was required prior to the building of the Nuffield United Services Officers Club in May 1951. The gate was then again relocated to its present (and final) position as the entrance to the cricket ground in Burnaby Road.

Above left: The stone-carved monogram dedicated to King James, can now be seen displayed in a tiny garden location in White Hart Road. One of an identical pair, they were originally built into the Camber Bastion. James the Second was King for three years only, 1685-1688. **Above right:** A rare (part-stereoscopic) view of the preserved anchor from H.M.S. *Victory*, shown displayed on a small stretch of foreshore at Old Portsmouth in 1852, until it was removed to its present location on a granite plinth at Clarence Promenade in 1887 by the Borough Engineer, H.Percy Boulnois.

Above: The 'evening' gun referred to previously was just one of a battery of twelve such guns maintained for use in the event of royal visits or other important occasions.

Left: This nineteenth-century engraving, however, suggests that the time signal had in Victorian times been discharged at mid-day from yet another location, that of the Kings Bastion.

Photographed in 1970, the view would be unrecognisable today. The location is in fact, the junction of French Street (Oyster Street of old) and White Hart Road. The triangular shaped area behind the chestnut fencing is that which was explored during the archaeological survey, revealing traces of cottages and the even earlier mediaeval dock

This even more remarkable photograph is that same triangular piece of land in 1939, when it housed the Royal Oak public house. The scene depicts an exercise involving members of the Auxiliary Fire Service demonstrating the use of a portable fire pump in the first weeks of the war. The Royal Oak together with almost all of this part of the old town was destroyed during the war.

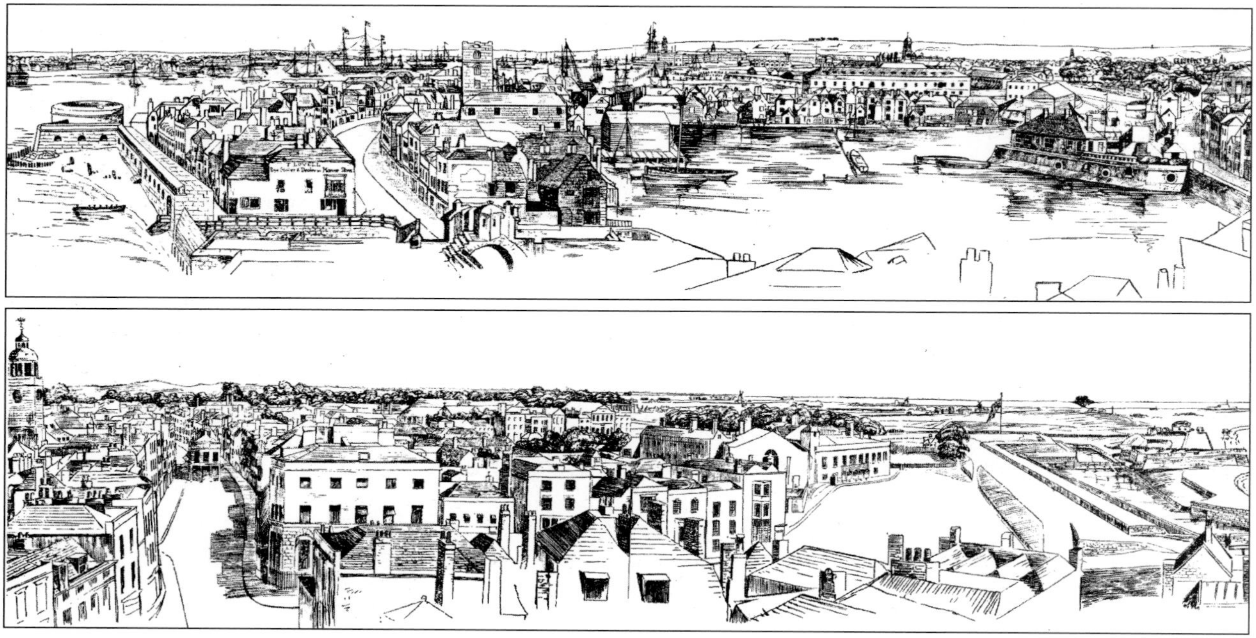

This panorama of Portsmouth as seen from the Semaphore, which formerly stood on the Square Tower, was sketched with painstaking accuracy by Admiral Spencer Smythe while in charge of the Signal Station in the early years of the nineteenth century.

Viewed from the sea, the west side of Point is set in a period following the First World War. To the left of centre is sited a structure with sliding steel shutters concealing a searchlight. This unit together with at least ten others lined the shore from here, eastwards almost to the South Parade Pier. In the event of a night attack from the sea, the Spithead approach to Portsmouth could be flooded with an intense light from these units.

This seascape includes the Semaphore Tower, which had been added to the Square Tower in the early nineteenth century. It was from here that messages could be sent via 14 Relay Stations, to the Admiralty in London. Skilled signallers, given clear weather conditions, could send or receive messages in as few as fifteen minutes.

The Square Tower minus the Semaphore had earlier served as Residence of the Governor, a beef store, an ammunition store and, in the 1880s, it had supported a massive water tank containing sea water which was used for washing the local streets, flushing the sewers and supplying the town's swimming pool and baths via a system of underground pipes.

Placed against the wall of the tower was once a bench dedicated to the memory of Sir Thomas Beecham who relaxed and enjoyed the sea air during a lunchtime break from rehearsals at the Portsmouth Guildhall. A commemorative plaque added following the death of Sir Thomas, listed the programme, which he conducted on this, his last ever concert performance.

In Memory of
Sir Thomas Beecham Bart, C.H.,
who conducted his last concert
At the Guildhall Portsmouth
May 7 1960
Overture, The Magic Flute.....Mozart
Symphony No 100 (Military)....Haydn
Suite, Love in Bath...Handel-Beecham
Symphony No 5...Schubert
On the River .... Delius
Bacchanale. ...Saint Saens
Royal Philharmonic Orchestra

Regrettably, both the bench and tribute have now been removed.

Richard Ford's achievements are legion; Mayor for two years, Guardian of the Portsea Union for eleven years, Solicitor, Director or Secretary of numerous local companies and, perhaps equally important to his interest in the hospital, Director of Public Health, for it was he who in 1862, advocated a system of drainage throughout the town. His memory is perpetuated in this very beautiful, brightly decorative fresco set into a recess in the Cathedral Church of Saint Thomas. The fresco, having the appearance of a stained glass window, depicts Christ healing the blind.

One of the town's hidden treasures can be discovered set in a wall bordering a path leading from Pembroke Road to the ramparts and Governors Green and, whilst age and condition fail to render it justice in a photograph, the tribute is self evident in this unusual equine memorial.

Close to this spot is buried
COMUS
A favourite pony given by
King William the IV
To
Lord Fred Fitzclarence
1832 died 1854 aged 25 years
Also
The CHIEF
A favourite old hunter given by
King William the IV
To
Lord Fred Fitzclarence
Aged 21 years
These horses were buried here by Lord Fred Fitzclarence
Relinquishing command of the south west-district
And Governorship of the fortress
1854

Portsmouth High Street c.1835. Having negotiated the narrow passage alongside the inconveniently sited Town Hall and Shambles, an outward-bound Mail Coach makes its way out of High Street where ladies gossip, window shop and make purchases in what was then the commercial and fashionable centre of town. Business and trades of all types operated from here, as can be seen from the following advertisements of the period.

PURVEYOR TO HIS ROYAL HIGHNESS THE DUKE OF CLARENCE,
YOUNG,
47, HIGH STREET,
Portsmouth.
Navy & Army supplied
with Live & Dead Stock,
Corn & Prefsed Hay,
CORNED BEEF,
Pickled & Dried Tongues.

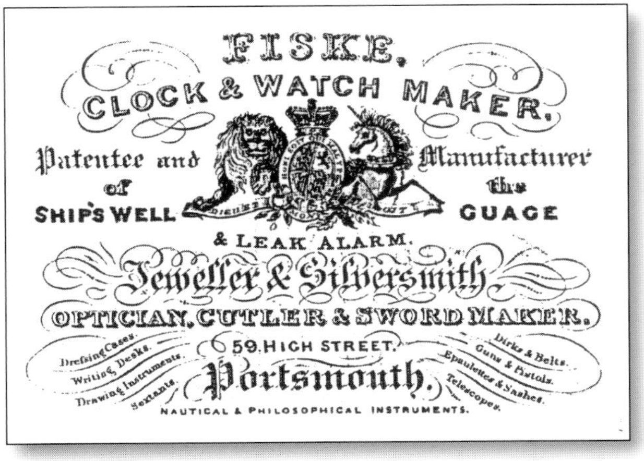
FISKE,
CLOCK & WATCH MAKER,
Patentee and Manufacturer
of the
SHIP'S WELL GUAGE
& LEAK ALARM.
Jeweller & Silversmith,
OPTICIAN, CUTLER & SWORD MAKER.
59, HIGH STREET,
Portsmouth.
Drefsing Cases.
Writing Desks.
Drawing Instruments.
Sextants.
Dirks & Belts.
Guns & Pistols.
Epaulettes & Sashes.
Telescopes.
NAUTICAL & PHILOSOPHICAL INSTRUMENTS.

T. H. FISKE,
82, High Street, Grand Parade,
PORTSMOUTH.
Furnishing & General Ironmonger,
Smith, Brazier, Tin-plate Worker, Locksmith,
BELL-HANGER &c.
Naval & Military Mefses.
completely furnished.
Ship & Yacht fittings, Guns,
Anchors, Chain Cables &c.
Dr. ARNOTT'S
STOVES.
SPERM OIL,
Argand & Candle Lamps
Superior Table Cutlery.
Kitchen Ranges, Stoves,
Improved Cooking Apparatus
Fire Irons Fenders &c.
Workmen sent to all parts of the Country.

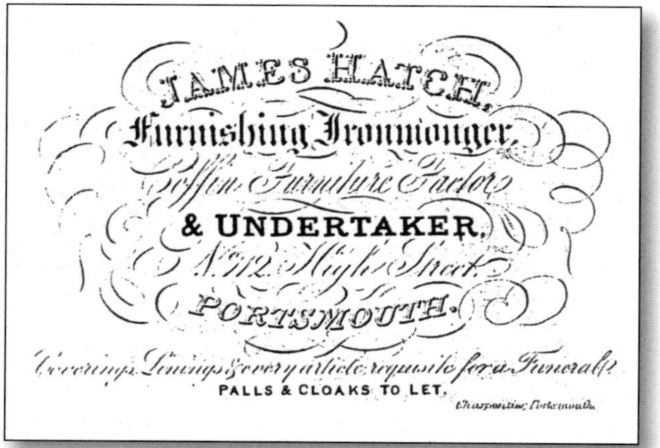
JAMES HATCH,
Furnishing Ironmonger,
Coffin Furniture Factor
& UNDERTAKER,
No. 112 High Street.
PORTSMOUTH.
Coverings, Linings & every article requisite for a Funeral.
PALLS & CLOAKS TO LET.

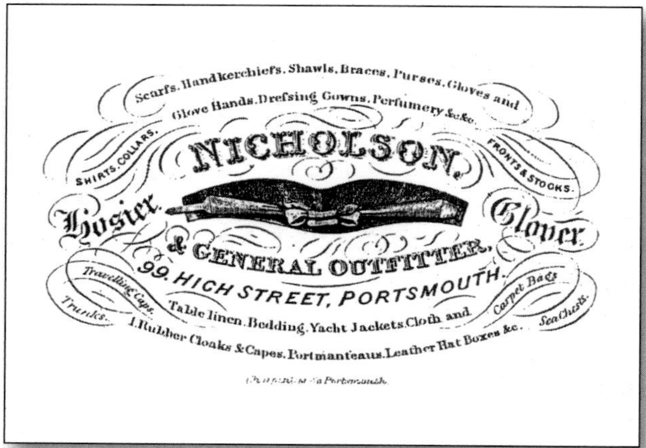
Scarfs. Handkerchiefs. Shawls. Braces. Purses. Gloves and
Glove Bands. Drefsing Gowns. Perfumery &c. &c.
SHIRTS. COLLARS.
FRONTS & STOCKS.
NICHOLSON,
Hosier.
Glover
& GENERAL OUTFITTER,
99. HIGH STREET, PORTSMOUTH.
Travelling Caps.
Trunks.
Table linen. Bedding. Yacht Jackets. Cloth and
I. Rubber Cloaks & Capes. Portmanteaus. Leather Hat Boxes &c.
Carpet Bags
Sea Chests.

GEO. STEBBING, SEN.R
Compafs Maker to H. M. Navy.
WHOLESALE & FOR
EXPORTATION
MANUFACTURER OF MATHEMATICAL & PHILOSOPHICAL INSTRUMENTS.
Agent for Chronometers
and Time Pieces.
Instruments Repaired & Adjusted
at a few Hours notice.
Optician & Instrument Maker
TO HER MAJESTY.
& HER ROYAL HIGHNESS THE DUCHESS OF KENT
AND THE ROYAL
YACHT SQUADRON.
66. High Street: Portsmouth
Agent for the Sale of Charts & Plans, Published by the Lords Commissioners of the Admiralty
GEORGE STEBBING, SEN. presents his best thanks to his friends and the public for the favours conferred on him during the last forty years, and will feel much obliged if they will be particular in directing to him at his Dwelling-House and Manufactory 66, HIGH STREET, (opposite the New Sally-Port), Portsmouth, or to his Branch Shop, 5, Common Hard, Portsea; as his eldest Son has opened a Shop, and being of the same Christian Name, it might be a serious injury to him, with so large a family, if the directions were not correct, as he has no connexion whatever with him or any other House in the County of Southampton, except, as above stated.

E. DAVIS.
Music & Musical Instrument Warehouse,
Music Seller By Appointment to the Royal Family.
HIGH STREET, PORTSMOUTH.

THE ROYAL WEDDING

In April 1662, Princess Catherine of the Portuguese Royal House of Braganza, set sail for England and her marriage to King Charles II. Due to storms and heavy seas, she did not arrive in Portsmouth until 14 May only to discover that Charles had been delayed on Parliamentary business and would not arrive in Portsmouth until the afternoon of 20 May. A contemporaneous engraving represents the Princess disembarking onto a raised causeway somewhere between the Round Tower and the Sallyport. After landing, Catherine entered her coach and drove round the principal streets of the town before retiring to apartments prepared for her in the residence of Portsmouth's military governor, which was attached to Domus Dei.

This early 19th century print shows the church and Governor's Residence joined almost as one building. Reading of the sizable entourage attending Her Royal Highness, the question must then be asked, where were they all accommodated? Surely not within the walls of the residence itself! The following list, taken from W.G.Gate's *Illustrated History of Portsmouth* describes the numbers involved and their particular function. 'Her suite was most outlandish. It consisted of more than one hundred persons including six Maids of Honour and a Governess to these extraordinary beauties. Besides these, there were six chaplains, four bakers, a Jew perfumer and a certain officer calling himself Her Highness's Barber.'

THE ORIGINAL GARRISON CHURCH.

Logistically, the Burghers of the town must have experienced problems in providing accommodation for one hundred 'high profile' guests particularly when the Governor's Residence was probably the only building of any size or substance in the town!

Far left: Portrait of Our Most Gracious Sovereign Lord King Charles the Second. By Sir Godfrey Kneller.

Left: Portrait of Her Royal Highness Princess Catherine of Braganza. By Dirck Stoop.

Our Most Gracious Soveraigne Lord
Charles the Second by the Grace of God King of Great
Brittaine France and Ireland Defender of the faith
And the most Illustrious Princesse ... Catarina Infanta of
Portugall daughter to the deceased Don Juan the ... Fourth and sister to the
present Don Alfonso King of Portugall were married at Portsmouth uppon thursday
the two & twentieth day of May in the yeere of our Lord God 1662 being in the fourteenth
yeere of his Majesties reigne by the Right Reverend Father in God Gilbert Lord Bishop of London Deane of his
Majesties Chappel Royall in the presence of severall of the Nobility of his Majesties dominions & of Portugall
Anno Domini 1662

Facsimile of the Marriage Certificate of King Charles the Second and Princess Catherine.

'Our Most Gracious Sovereign Lord, Charles the II by the grace of God, King of Great Britain, France and Ireland, Defender of faith, etc. and the most illustrious Princess Donna Caterina, Infanta of Portugal, daughter of the deceased Don Juan IV and sister of the present Don Alfonso, King of Portugal, were married at Portsmouth upon Thursday the two and twentieth day of May, in the year of our Lord God 1662, being in the fourteenth year of his Majesty's reign; by the Right Reverend Father in God Gilbert, Lord Bishop of London, Dean of his Majesty's Chapel Royal in the presence of several of the Nobility of his dominions and of Portugal. Anno Domini 1662.'

PORTSEA ISLAND
Harbour and Environs

'A view of the Town and Harbour of Portsmouth,' is from an engraving dated 1723.

An illustrated volume dedicated to the old town, must include this most interesting panorama of Portsmouth and its environs. The town itself occupied just a small corner of Portsea Island at the harbour entrance; the remainder of the island is devoid of any major settlements at this time and, those that are seen will later develop into the villages of Fratton, Buckland and Copnor. The early church of St Mary's Portsea can be detected as can Southsea Castle. Across the Harbour, Gosport Town appears to be developing 'ribbon' fashion whilst, together with neighbouring Portsmouth, shipping dominates the harbour mouth and shoreline.

The panorama, sketched from the slopes of Portsdown Hill, shows Portchester Castle commanding an overall view of the harbour and its approaches, as it has done since Roman times. Mudflats within the northwest reaches of the harbour were later to be reclaimed and are today Whale, Horsea and Little Horsea Islands.

PUBS, TAVERNS, INNS AND ALE HOUSES OF PORTSMOUTH – 1716
A Postscript by Russsell T. Fox

The one-only illustration in this postscript is that of a traditional pint tankard, mug or jug, commonly used in the early pubs, taverns, inns and alehouses of Old Portsmouth.

Salt-glazed stoneware tankards became popular during the late seventeenth century after the English potteries had perfected production techniques in this medium, reaching a peak of demand during the eighteenth century, notably in the period c.1730-1770. Stoneware was ideally suitable for use as tavern tankards as it was (and still is) a particularly robust fabric which, once glazed, proves impervious to almost all liquids, with the exception of certain acids, e.g. fluoric.

The most recognisable feature of these stoneware tankards was their overall finish, usually in brown or two-tone brown. In the case of the two-tone variety the lower part of the body could be of a light to mid-brown, the upper body was usually darker brown. This was achieved by applying an iron-rich wash to the upper part prior to firing, the more iron the wash contained, the darker the resulting finish: the origin of 'The Little Brown Jug'. The owner of a tavern would order a quantity of tankards from a particular pottery and, by request, have his name and the name of his establishment appended to his vessels.

It is a well-recorded fact that Old Portsmouth has always had more than its fair quota of establishments offering liquid refreshment for retail. Written records of these taverns, inns and ale houses etc. are to be found in the many registers, corporate documents and legal proceedings accounts of the time. From these records such details as the location and name of a particular establishment and the name and details concerning the respective proprietor can be ascertained through patient research.

Full use of these resources has been made here to establish the pedigree of a selection of tankards bearing documentary evidence recovered from various parts of Old Portsmouth in recent years through archaeological investigation and research. This research has also revealed a social and historical picture of the drinking habits of the male (and female) population of the town over several centuries.

The illustration is of a beer jug from David Duckett's tavern The Antelope, which in 1876 was located at Number 7 The Parade, Old Portsmouth.

The Antelope, a relative latecomer to the scene, does not appear in local records prior to, or after the above date although licensed premises bearing the name Antelope are later recorded in Hanover Street Portsea.

From this time on, in the old town at least, the number of taverns and beer houses was on the decline. In a small town of less than one mile square, saturation point must have been reached when in 1716, the number of such premises totalled 69.

The following list, researched in detail from records within the City archives shows the street, name of premises and innkeeper's name.

In HIGH STREET, THE PARADE and lanes adjoining

The Bull's Head	John Carleton
The Prince George's Head	Mr Howard
The George	Owen Rock
The Three Compasses	Mr Reeves
The Flower Pot	Mr Price
The Dolphin	William Gray
The Three Tuns and Lanthorns	John Mooring
The Magpie	Edward Edwards
The Two Fighting Cocks	Joseph Neale
The Two Fencing Masters	Mr Harris
The Wagon and Lamb	Mrs Hays
The Fortune of War	John Wheeler
The Thistle and Crown	Mr Olcorn
The Scotch Arms	Mrs Lensley

The White Horse	Peter Querell
The Three Crowns	Mrs Stanmoor
The White Hart	Mr Grigg
The Golden Lion	Thomas Welstead
The Dog and Duck	Mr Drue
The Eight Bells	Mr Ragg
The Three Tuns	Mr Walden
The Red Lion	John West

OYSTER STREET

The Roebuck	Christopher Levett
The Crowne	Thomas Wattell
The Bell	Jonathan Brett
The Plume and Feathers	Luke Smith
The Bakers' Arms	John Jones

ST THOMAS'S STREET

The Joyners' Arms	Widow Roberts
The Goate	William Hellyer
The King's Arms	William Neville

ST MARY'S STREET

The Plough	Thomas Gamblin
The Anchor and Crown	Thomas Holt
The Three Horseshoes	Henry Tarrant

WARBLINGTON STREET

The Peacock	William Bates
The Talbott	George Barkham
The Bricklayer's Arms	Edward Forbes
The King's Head	Widow Rose
The London Prentice	Jasper Skelton

'HOUSES WITHOUT POINT GATE' (Broad Street etc.)

The Ile of Wite Hige (Hoy)	Tobye Dreake
The Bricklayer's Arms	Nickolas Pearson
The London	George Gessedge
The King's Head	John Sumerset
The Union	William Hopkence
The Dolphin	William Donkson
The Union	William Drew
The Fortune of War	Thomas Werson
The Rose and Crown	George Wynshyn
The Nors Toy	Thomas Colance
The Cross Keys	Robert Borsell
The King's Head	John Smith
The Five Bells	John Doane
The Fishing Hige (Hoy)	Elizabeth Cole
The Globe	Edward Garit
The Orange Tree	Mary Hoahence
The Last	Abraham Williams
The Black Dog	Jane Grear
The Black Swan	John Potten
The Thistle and Crown	Samuel Wawe
The Blew Post	Seaben Cole
The George	John Anderson
The Golden Hart	John Foster
The Crown	Robert Douglas

The Three Guns	George White
The Seven Stars	Matthew Camuel
The Greyhound and Last	Richard Smith
The Row-Barge	Charles Robarts
The Plymouth Arms	John Wessell
The Bell	Thomas Holt
The Southampton Hige (Hoy)	Robert Treadgal

This staggering list naming all 69 such premises in the town should be compared with a survey taken in this year 2006, when only 10 licensed premises were recorded. This at a time when visitors from Greater Portsmouth and tourists from elsewhere swell the number of resident drinkers to well exceed the population figures of the year 1716.